A Cup of Coffee
with a Side of Feelings

A Pocket Book of Poetry

By Epiphany Recker

Table of Contents

I want you to fold my book, crease my book, dog-ear and bookmark and highlight and use it as a coaster, but in case you wish your copy to stay pristine, here is a somewhat literate Table of Contents.

At the Beginning ~ I'm Sorry ~ Crumbling Beneath Me ~ Rebirth ~ Eat Dirt ~ The Witch ~ Fight ~ Hold Me ~ I Used to Be ~ At the Bottom ~ I'm Trying ~ The Stained-Glass ~ Lovely Girl ~ Crush ~ Butterfly ~ Old Light ~ Thoughts ~ Blue Raven Wilds ~ Time Lost ~ I Think My Dog is a Dragon ~ Defeat it ~ Passing the Torch ~ The Siren's Song ~ Leftovers ~ Comfort ~ Trudging ~ Onward ~ Don't Look Back ~ With Me Nightly ~ New Light ~ Relief ~ If I Can, I Must ~ Insects ~ Loving Match ~ Monsters in the Dark ~ You're Beautiful ~ Arrogant Poet ~ Here's to Love ~ Wait for Me ~ This is Where I Come From ~ Old Friend, Was Friend ~ There was a Moon ~ Amayata ~ AlphaBorb ~ The Meaning of Life ~ Moonlight Wander ~ Stuck ~ Failing is Success ~ Inspiration ~ Life ~ Greed ~ Am I? ~ I Am. ~ A Place of Sin ~ Myself ~ The Beginning After ~ Work

Commute ~ Down ~ Blue ~ Cold ~ Nameless Fear ~ Me, Not Me ~ Said What? ~ Colour in the Wood ~ The Grinning Crow ~ Choice ~ Pain, Gain, Sweat Stain ~ The Void ~ Winter's Gone ~ Clothes ~ To you I am? ~ I Saw That Day ~ Shared Memories ~ No Shoes ~ Wolves ~ Power ~ My Art ~ My Journey ~ It's All Gone

~ Friends and Family ~

Ferryman ~ The Void Beckons ~ Dead Garden ~ Me, Me. ~ To the newly discovered x-ray lights from behind the far side of a black hole 800 million light years away proving the theory that immense concentrations of matter can bend the fabric of spacetime

Introduction

I spent a long time trying to decide what to write as an introduction and I enjoyed most of what I wrote. However, it all felt a bit grand and pretentious to be at the start of a simple book of poetry. All of it, accept this one sentiment from the point of view of the book itself.

"My dream is to live in a coat pocket, where someone will pull me out and read a little of me for comfort. To be sat on, be dog-eared, be cherished and loved. Wherever I end up, I hope I am enjoyed." - A Pocket Book of Poetry

At the Beginning

Beach Chalk,
Concrete Walls,
Jam,

A fence, locked,
A tree inside,

Music playing,
Moving forward,
But I couldn't see,

At the beginning there is hope,
But after hope,
If you don't hold on,
It's gone,

At the Beginning.

I'm Sorry

I'm sorry I didn't have a leaf that one time,

I'm sorry that I didn't have a leaf,

I just wanted a picture.

Crumbling Beneath Me

Standing on the earth as it crumbles beneath me,

For some they rejoice and for some they may cry, but me,

I remember the good days of times past,
The things we shared the memories will last,

And the times that I missed you,

The times you were gone,
But you always return after not too long,

The blue sky above us when you were mine,
The night that preceded it for so short a time,

The morning after the night before, you were gone,
Why did it end, what did I do wrong?

I was in your chair, reading as if I didn't care,
The door opened and I saw you were there,

But you were not alone...

Suddenly the earth crumbled beneath me,

Some rejoiced and some they cried,

As for me,

I have died.

Rebirth

To valley our stomachs when food is of no use to us,
And when water is rusted like copper in the cold,

When life has lost its value,
When fibrous profit has taken hold,
And rooted our feet in a jealous mind,

To overwhelm us in the future,
And frighten us of our past,

A voice will stand out,
Soft,
Pure,
And full of purpose,

But whether or not we listen,
Will result in water's revival,
Food sources replenished,

And from the Stone Age we rise to conquer the growing evil of corrupted hearts,

It's blackened politics of greed and lust,

To break its banner we must hold firm,

We must stand tall,

And in all famous the words,
"Fight for the soul of our nation."

Until the structure of our homes, our work
and families become relevant again,

A rebirth, a restoration,
A reconstruction, but the question remains,

Do we fix what is broken?
Or,
Do we tear it down and start again?

Eat Dirt

My life was nothing to support him,

The no good monstrosity grim,

Total heart slaughter with a cleaver,

All his mind was telling him to do was,

"Leave Her"

The world is better off with one less fool,

It won't be me, but,

I'll stand and watch as your body decomposes,

Into soil and dust,

Probably sooner rather than later,

And don't cry for help,

Because I won't,

Eat the dirt pile you lay in.

The Witch

There once were two children who wandered
too far,
wandered too far,
wandered too far,

There once were two children who wandered
too far,

Oh no, their souls,
Oh no, their souls,

They entered the dark forest black and all
green,
black and all green,
black and all green,

They entered the dark forest all black and all
green,

Oh no, their souls,
Oh no, their souls,

They found a house so small and so sweet,
small and so sweet,
small and so sweet,

They found a house so small and so sweet,

> Oh no, their souls,
> Oh no, their souls,

Upon their knock an old lady answered,
an old lady answered,
an old lady answered,

Upon their knock an old lady answered,

> Oh no, their souls,

> Oh no, their souls,

She let them in for cakes and sweets,
cakes and sweets,
cakes and sweets,

She let them in for cakes and sweets,

> Oh no, their souls,
> Oh no, their souls,

Once they were plump she tried to bake them,
Tried to bake them,
Tried to bake them,

Once they were plump she tried to bake them,

>Oh no, their souls,
>Oh no, their souls,

In their fright they tossed her into,
>Tossed her into,
>Tossed her into,

In their fright they tossed her into,

>The red hot oven,
>The red hot oven,

From that house they fled so fast,
>Fled so fast,
>Fled so fast,

From that house they fled so fast,

Leaving the charcoaled old lady behind,

Safe and sound they speak not a word,
>Speak not a word,
>Speak not a word,

Safe and sound they speak not a word.

Fight

Call upon your saviour,
Hope they hear the call,

For the time has come,
The war to end all wars,

Fight for yourself,
Fight for family,
Fight for friends,

Fight to the end.

Hold Me

Be my rock,
Hold me firm,
I can not see,
The pale wind shakes the trees,

My tail whips,
My hair flips,
As I wait for you,
The water is cold without your arms,

I hear your voice,
I seek your tone,
I feel the keys,
That melody warm and smooth like river stones,

Keep me calm,
Know my heart,
I love your soul,
I shall be with you, even when we part,

Be my rock,
Hold me firm,
Steal my skin,
Seal my love.

I Used to Be

I used to be a girl.
Feminine and beautiful, but modest and shy.

I used to be a guy.
Male and handsome(averagely so), "one of the guys".

I used to be stable.
Able to function like the average kid on the block.

I used to be whole.
No broken bones, no pain and no scars.

I used to be healthy.
No trauma, no defects, no crutches, no sickness cept hay fever.

I used to be human.
No unusual needs, no inhuman feeding, no darkness in the brain.

I used to be clean.
No stains, no dirt, no grime, no sludge, no mud...

I used to be, but now look at me.

At the Bottom

Devastation,
My lungs, weak and small,
The world around me dire,

I can feel them,
The nibbling,
Like pinpricks of fire,

Douse me in gasoline,

This will not stand,
But the rocks beneath me,
Are as loose as sand,

Sail,
Torn Sail,

Run,
My feet bleed,

The soreness tears at the heart of my fight,
I am not slain,

Exhaustion,
Sorrow,

I am going to fall,
One way or another,

The depths of my tears,
That of a salt water lake,

A hole,
I am trapped,

But there is always further to fall,

I am not defeated,
But I must rest awhile,

At the bottom.

I'm Trying

The eyes that shroud,
The eyes that cloud,
The eyes that waver,
Nothing left to savour,

Things must be seen,
Things must be said,
Is morality, respect and kindness dead?

An act portrayed as greedy or selfish,
Is nothing to my soul, it's selfless,

Concern and care,
I ask for nothing in return,
Met with a cold stare,
Met with silent burn,

A mask, A cast,
A show, A farce,

For all I try to give my heart,

And even though my intention good,
Still I am met with hate, misunderstood,

Take these words to heart,
Take this statement wish,

To show and give a handsome dish,
Of love and care, sweet and kind,

For the little hope I have to find,
Please hear my words,
This is true,

My wish is only to be nice to you.

Lovely Girl

My music taste has always been patchwork,
My Lyrics without tune,
My music without words,
My poetry uneven with no cords,

But there is one melody that makes me smile,
One that sores without wings, and reads well whatever the tempo,

Silly and cute,
Funny and sweet,

A tune worth keeping around,
Worthy of platinum and blue ribbon,
Number one!

Melody, a sweet song,
A perfect mix of melancholy and merriment,
No lyrics to sing,
No tune to hum,
But the prettiest of any song...

Melody

Crush

It's a swell beneath the chest,
A racing in the breast,

A flood through the gates,
What love creates,

Held fast at the feet,
For them to approach,
To greet,

Your tongue tied,
Yourself eyed,

And soon you are on your knees,
Hearing your own pleas,

Pray save me from this torment,
One way or another.

Old Light

Oh, the falling of life that seems to plague me so,
I would melt if that would help, but yet it holds me still.

That darkness collides with my inner skin,
I try so hard to let it out and not keep it in.

To those who had time to care at my side,
Some I know well, and some from the blue,
I thank you,

I cherish your words of love or even shared woes,
I thank you for helping me live a little longer,
With the weight, Oh, the heavy weight I can not seem to leave behind.

My darkness seemed to cloud his life when he was here,
And now that he has gone to the light,

He left me without it, my darkness was to his light,
I am left in the dark it seems, without a light to stand by,

Oh how I wish I could see it, that smile again,
Feel myself in his arms,
Be held close as I wept,
I wish to see him once more.

The only thing that keeps me here,
is my polar companion that I hold so dear.

She sits here in the dark with me, sharing my weight,
Though I wish her no pain, I am glad that she is here.

Thank you to all, may your days be bright,
and I may soon join you, soon, in the light.

Thoughts

What thoughts we ponder in the night's solitude,

What flourishes we word ourselves in an attempt to bring about intelligence,

What sounds we speak when none will listen,

What meanings we make when all feel invulnerable.

Blue Raven Wilds

In the Wilds of the Blue,
I walk the Swamp and Marshland through,

In hopes to spot a fearsome sight,
Of which I see in the dead of Night,

The gorgeous creatures that stalk,
Tall with a long-striding walk,

Where most fear to tread,
The Wilds of the Blue may ye dread,

Named of themselves,
The Blue Raven Elves.

Time Lost

Too many, Too late,
Smudging a clean slate,

No matter how I clean,
Traces still can be seen,

An old black board,
Washed to the core,

Unbreakable and Unmendable,
Unforgettable and Unforgivable,

Too late to undo,
The years of trust in you,

So many a chance,
So that we could advance,

But still you decree,
To rip the faith from me,

Leave me breathless,
Leave me bleeding,
The emotion only left seeding,

Regret.
Give me my time back... Please.

I Think My Dog is a Dragon

I think my dog is a dragon and nobody else knows but me. He's black and shiny and furry on the outside, but that is all a sham.

When no one else is looking, his fur turns into slick green scales and his head grows horns. So I'm beginning to think that he's not a dog at all.

He barks like a dog, but when he sleeps he snorts like a pig. When he runs he huffs and puffs like a wolf. And at night when no one is watching, he snaps and clamps and chops and stomps, breathing fire all about. He melted my crayons right into the carpet. Of course, I had to take the blame.

I'm pretty sure my dog is a dragon. 'Cause when no one is around, he grows so big that he has to hide under the deck. He tucks his wings under him and scorches the ground making himself a nice warm nest.

I'll bet you anything my dog is a dragon, because when my mom turns away his tail grows long and pointy and he grows spines up his back. But of course my mom never sees that.

My dog isn't a dog at all and I know 'cause when my dad leaves the room, his snout gets all scaly, his tongue splits like a snake's and his teeth grow longer and sharper than knives.

I tell ya, it's quite wonderful when you're trying to sleep at night and your dog stretches into a massive dragon and curls peacefully around your bed.

I think my dog is a dragon, but I don't mind. He's shiny and sweet and tidy and neat and no one suspects a thing.

Defeat it

Harbinger of the moon,
Keeper of the soul,

We walk the streets of black,
Beyond the reach of light,

When we travel,
We must be prepared,

For whatever is ahead,
What could drive us to fear,
To panic us dead,

Rewind your terror,
Seek the key,

For the heart of adventure,
Lies within your skin,

And the heart of horror,
Lives within your soul,

Defeat it.

Passing the Torch

Help the weak and help the strong,

No one does it when you're gone,

When in need we seek a friend,

Throw you away and start again,

Here's to the common people,

Fighting against everyday evil,

Day by day we move along,

Just to get by,

When do we ask for help,

The help we heed,

But wait to receive,

A friend that we are in need.

And yet that person so blinded by greed,

Ignores you.

The Siren's Song

The Siren, she calls
The Sea, it sings
And as I sail on the warning bell rings,

To be caught in a storm is a thing we all fear,
And the doldrums for a seaman is a worthy test,

But nothing compares,
To the hypnotising stares,
Of a siren out at sea,

Beware of the siren my lad,
For it is not a kiss she seeks,

It's a man's strong chest,
A fluttering heart, at unrest,
She'll hold you firm and pull you beneath,

But until you lay dead from gore,
Far down upon the ocean floor,

Only then will you find relief.
Beware, Beware.

Leftovers

Could and Should are one in the same,

If one has the money, if one has the means,

I have neither, but new found holes in my concrete jeans,

If only I could bathe,

If so, perhaps I would not feel my situation so grave,

I am left to my own devices in this state,

My feast is the yeast built up on your discarded plate.

Comfort

I am water, I am rain,
I drench you in calm,
Much needed sadness,

You were in need of a good cry,
Swim in my river and no one shall see your tears,

Wade in my waves,
Feel my touch upon your soft skin,

Close your eyes, feel the drizzle of rain on your face
As my surface carries you into peace,

Rest easy, you are in good hands,
My hold is strong, my current can be swift,
But my touch is soft and knowing,
My song sweet and relaxing,

I hold your hand in this wet,
Though neither wet nor cold shall bother us,
For we are warm with each other,

We are water, we are rain.

Trudging Onward

They are fully grown,
Blooming in the throws of early spring,

But they're falling,
Falling away into a watery grave,
Dumbfounded.

"You know I don't want to do this, it's just my job."...

Fall behind, ready and power through,
Try to stop my roaring flames,
As they burn the roses right out of your hands,

We're closed.

Drip,
Feel,
Fall.

Don't Look Back

Has that have left, of motions past,

The line of struggle, previously last,

Among the ashes, time due fight,

Of life the elder, without strife,

Complete in vision, too tremendous to pass,

For long emerged rest, of laughing mass,

Compose us all, without anger entrusted.

With Me Nightly

With me nightly is my blanky,
Cozy cuddly, warm and snuggly,

With me nightly is my water,
Cup of thirsty, wet and spilly

With me nightly is my hanky,
In case of sniffling, sneezing and wheezing,

With me nightly is my night light,
To keep me safe; it's soft and luminous,

With me nightly is my teddy,
Squishy, fluffy, soft and scruffy,

And with me nightly is my bubey,
Holding me happily, arms around me,

With me Nightly.

New Light

Upon the sidewalk rain it drizzles,
Speckled with polka dots until it's dark and grey,
But inside I am, with your hand in mine,
The rain bothers me not with you by my side,

Wash away my pain,
Dry my tears,
Hold me close,
Chase away my fears,

When I'm with you, nothing else I can see,
When I'm with you, the world dissolves around me,
When I'm with you, my heart soars higher than the sky,
When I'm with you, happiness is the only thing to make me cry,

In this rain I see you, a drizzle to downpours,
Lightning it flashes,
Thunder it roars,
And I'm sure my shoes have holes,

But I feel not the wet,

And I feel not the cold,
When I have you to hold.

Relief

Annalise had a rope,
She pulled,
And pulled,
And pulled,
And pulled,
Then one day she forgot what she was pulling,
And why she was pulling it,
So,
She let go.

If I Can, I must

With hope and help I lend my ears,
To the deaf,
To the blind,
To those beyond my years,

And with my touch release your tear,
A guardian of happiness,

Destroyer of fears,

Feed the hungry,
Heal the ailing,

With what I do there can be no failing,

Strength, my friend,
Help me through another day,

Wisdom, my weapon,
Keep me sharp, do not decay,

Motivation, my need,
My will to fight,

Those horrors and terrors that go bump in the night.

Sated

The sleep, and be sated,
For the world,
at glance,
May never be better for it.

Insects

Under the sun we are silly and fun,
However, sometimes you have to be wary,

Let's talk about it shall we.

Most of us are harmless, but you should
always be cautious,

Look, but don't touch without an adult.

Because we may look friendly or pretty, but
that can be misleading.

Ladybugs, Butterflies, Worms, Moths and
Snails, are the friendliest of all of us.

Ladybugs
I can be red or yellow with cute little black
spots and I love to eat leaves.
If you put me in a box, put holes in the top so
that I can breathe.

Butterflies
We can be all colours, shapes and sizes. We
are full of surprises.

Even though our wings look soft, please don't touch them.
And If you see us in a tree, sleeping in a pea, please, please leave us be.

Worms

We're wirly and curly, slimy and squirrely,
Munch on dirt, and dig away,
But come to the surface when it rains,

But remember we are the friendly ones and don't mind you,
But some are grumpy and would rather be alone,

So be careful, and cautious,
When in doubt leave us out.

Loving Match

Sadness looms under grey clouds,
Which do their part,
Casting shadows over a heavy heart,

Release me from my madness,
If it is not one thing,
It is another,

My work,
My days,
My nights,
My other,

Sweet thing you thaw a frozen soul,
Although I confess, I see not your goal,

To release me,
To recage me,
I do not know,

What knowledge I have is that you are as
gentle as new falling snow,

You, my lover,
You my match,

Healing my heart,
A rip to its patch,

Stay my beloved and never leave,
For in your loss,
I will not but grieve,

You are my only,
I will say it once and say it again,
Eternal life with you I'll spend.

Monsters in the Dark

The lights that flicker
The window that never stays shut
The door that never stays locked
The monster under the bed
The prayers that sate no demons
The lights that never stay lit

To find yourself face to face with fear.

You're Beautiful

It's okay to be lumpy and frumpy,
Round and squishy,
Short and fluffy,

Cause you may be surprised to find,
That what everyone loves,
Is on the inside.

Arrogant Poet

Without merit,
here I sit,
Squawking out drivel,
Like a tune deaf parrot,

Here's to Love

Here's to love, the spire of all emotion,
Here's to love, a feeling as large as the ocean,
Here's to love, a path not easily chosen,
And here's to love, a link not so easily broken.

Wait for Me

It's a big world and I'm getting scared,
Don't know how people do it,
Don't know how to be prepared,

I see people younger than me succeed,
I see everyone rising peacefully,
And I think "What about me?".

This is Where I Come From

I come from old forests,
Concrete forests,
Raccoons 'n coyotes,

From wet pavements,
Wets slugs,
Worms and snails,

From autumn leaves,
Fir trees,
Horse chestnuts 'n chestnuts,

From dogs 'n cats,
From juice boxes and snacks,

From soccer balls,
Ice cream stalls,

This is where I come from, and I wouldn't
have it any other way.

I come from homemade root beer,
And from bubbly apple juice,

From bikes 'n cars,
Scooters and monkey bars,

From dirt 'n sticks,
From a creative fix,
And I wouldn't have it any other way,

I come from sideways glances,
And whispers behind hands,

From curled in corners,
From outstretched hands,

From hospitals, therapy and dreaming,
From family,
From friends,
From my wife,
From hope,

This is where I come from and I wouldn't have it any other way.

Old Friend, Was Friend

I only saw you one last time,
And I don't think I thought of you as you,
I was mad,
And no one was there,
So I followed my needing,
And it lead me to the nowhere of you,

Before I could explain,
Before I could say,
You were leaving,
And I would see you no more,

The last time I saw you,
Was the first time in a long time,
And you closed the door.

There Was a Moon

There was a moon,
And then there wasn't,
It was gone,

Like the grass and tree,
Like the stairs and the gravel,

Like the chestnuts,
And those spiky red berries that were yellow inside,

There was a moon,
And then,
It was gone.

Amayata

Amayata legs of three,
Sitting in a cherry tree,

Amayata pray for me,
Oh Amayata pray for me,

Amayata God of Light,
Flying high above my kite,

Amayata legs of three,
Won't you pray for me.

AlpheBorb

Andy the Alphaborb accepts Alligator addition.

Betty the Bord bets better than bulldogs.

Chris the Cardinal communicates contentment about his cage.

Douglas the Dove Demonstrates Devilish Decisions.

Esther the Emu emanates energy while engaging elephants.

Fred the Feathery friend flutters frantically.

Gwen the Goose glorifies grass with goslings. (Rolling around in the grass w/ babies)

Harry the Honker honks horrendously after hoarding.

Ingrid the Ibis illustrated as interesting images.

Jared the Jay jumps joyously about jaguars.

Kerry the Kestrel kicks keys, that killjoy.

Landon the Lark lounges luxuriously with the leopards.

Mandy the Magpie mocks the Monarchy.

Nigel the Nightingale's Nana nitpicks his nest.

Olivia the Owl orbits the oaks at odd hours.

Patrick the Parrot parades his plume proudly.

Quimbey the Quail quivers questioningly over quiche.

Roger the Raven respectfully ransacks rubbish.

Selene the Stern swims swiftly and smoothly.

Thomas the Tawny tattle tails on turtles tactlessly.

Ursula the Unicorn ungulates urgently.

Vincent the Vulture views a variety of victims.

Wendy the Woodpecker wishes she was a whale.

Xander the Borb X-Rays xylophones.

Yellow Yolanda unyieldingly yodels.

Zoey the Zealot Zeroes in on Zero.

The Meaning of Life

Just think,
If you think, you can plan,
If you plan, you can do,
If you do, you can move,
If you move, you can move forward,
If you move forward,

You can finally stand still.

Moonlight Wander

Shall we hide

Shall we dance among the gravestones hither,
and thither and beyond,

Shall we think upon a stone,

Watch through a window,

His dog, and his bone.

Stuck

It's hope you hold when life feels distance,
It's pain you feel when it's too close,

You feel suffocated and incoherent,
As if you said a thousand words and no one heard you,

What can come of this?
This endless speech,

A time long past of meaningless, or meaningful time,
And yet, when the end comes,
It feels like nothing happened at all.

Failing is Success

Much like my life, my keyboard is all a-blur,
If only I knew the future ahead, if only I knew for sure,

But such is life to not know,
For the unknown goes to show,

That in the end we can say "We Did",
Instead of that "We Tried".

Inspiration

Sideways the earth moves,
When one waits for the moon to set,
Or rise,
When the great tortoise lumbers through the starry expanse,
The moon follows, the sun follows,
the universe parts like a raging river fearful of a powerful boulder.

Life

Just think,
If you think, you can plan,
If you plan, you can do,
If you do, you can move,
If you move, you can move forward,
If you move forward,

You can finally stand still.

Greed

The purest rivers run with silver,
The darkest streams are stained with gold,
Be careful what you pan for,
For greed will rot your soul.

Am I?

It's quite a thing,
To be and not be,
To be of a stranger's choice,
Or to not be anyone,

A stranger, to make it break you,
It takes one,
One makes many,
And then you are done,

But is it a someone you want to be?
A someone depending on the opinions of strangers,
Or no one, who is someone to a select few,
A few that care,

So who are you?
Someone... or someone else?

I Am.

I am what I am,
and beyond itself confined,

The structure of will,
ever collapsing under the weight of
expectations,

The cast, on coming disaster,
The theatre, a never ending drama,

It plays out for unwelcome scornful eyes,
To resist is to be tired, so I fall,

But I must also carry on,

For, I am what I am,
and beyond itself, set free.

A Place of Sin

Unbeknownst to him,
A feathered frame, against the harsh,
unforgiving cold of the underworld,
The residue he trodden,

The husk for hissing shale that once was the
devil's playground, his prison,
A place of belittlement, once burning with the
white hot flames of betrayal.

Now a blackened, charcoal waste.

Myself

My bun has never done up when I want it,
It does up unexpectedly for me to cherish,

My eyes have never seen what I've wanted,
They see things in the wanting and I oblige,
Sometimes,

My ears have heard too much,
To which my mouth has no more to say,

So I sit here on my chair,
In a state of becoming,

While my hands write,
And my bun done up unexpectedly.

The Beginning After

There was a room,
There was a door,
There was a dresser,
There was a drawer,

There was a book,
There was a store,

In stepped a girl,
Out stepped a lady,

Too soon,
Too fast,
A new mind,
A new grasp,

The world is different,
The world is bright,
With new eyes that see,
A different sight.

Shall We

Shall we hide

Shall we dance among the gravestones,
hither, thither and beyond,

Shall we think upon a stone,

Watch through a window,

His dog, and his bone.

Work Commute

It can walk me in fur-lined boots through an old viking village. Trudging through the snow.

It can drape me in a victorian gown, decorated with bows and lace and frills, on my way to a ball.

It dangling a headdress to my ears and a foot above my head from an ancient culture long dead.

Every car is a horse drawn carriage every building a modist, a tea shop, a saloon.

Every home is a castle or manor.

Every highway a river.

Every stubble I suffer is on an uneven cobblestone in the past.

Every taste on my tongue is time.

Down

I'm going down,
where the fish don't swim,
I'm going down,
where the sinners sin,
I'm going down,
to meet all my foes,
I'm going down,
with seaweed between my toes,

I'm not a saint,
But I'm no sinner,
Filled with hate,
And half-eaten dinner,
I don't wanna fall,
But I've got no choice,
For my time has come,
And I can hear his voice,

Blue

Slate, Stone, a coffin to hold one's emotions away from the light.

Sky, A dreamer, a goal to find and reach. Navy, youth, clothes, growth.

Ocean, a wide expanse to fill with all that we can spill.

Sapphire, bright, sparkling and beaming.

Midnight, the calm, recharge.

Powder, an expression, a personal one

Persian, a purveyor of public knowledge.

Periwinkle, a flower to admire and pick in spring.

Baby, there was a time, before this time, before now.

Azure, beautiful, on the inside, on the outside, shiny or matte. Beauty.

Cold

I was far out. Out on the ice. On a hill, a mountain in a basin.

It was a basin, but I didn't know that's what it was called.
It was wetlands, but all I knew was that it was land and it was wet.
It was a forest, but it was just trees,

I could see the harsh land, the withered land under the snow.

The unforgiving ice blanketing the unforgiving desert.

And I will be cold.
If not my feet, then my hands,
if not my hands, then my ears,
If not my ears, then my heart,

My heart will remain frozen and stagnate no matter the season.

Nameless Fear

It matters not the timeless past,
A growing moon in a darkness vast,

We seek knowledge whole,
Whilst some cast out soul,

The meaning is clear,
What we fear,

Is all.

Me, not Me

Then,
It's my face,
Not clean, but not pocked,

It's my body,
Not slim, but fit,

It's my mind,
Not anyone else's,

Again,
It's my face,
No makeup, not pretty,

It's my body,
Not thin, not right,

It's my mind,
Not normal, too different

Now,
It's my face,
Not clean enough,
Not young enough,

It's my body,

Not thin enough,
Not fit enough,
Not right,

It's my mind,
Not normal enough,
Not focused enough,
Muddled,

It was to me,
It was to them,

And because of them it is to me,
Mine, not mine,

Not right, not even now.

Said what?

He said,
She said,
Hear say,

Say this.
What stories can I tell to blank walls across from empty shelves?

Are my points even points,
If there is no one to hear them?
She said,

If I am already the "Bad Guy" what good is being good?
He said,

But then, the words I write are just that, words,

And I don't know them well enough to even spell them,

So why would anyone hear what I have to say?

We are Enough

It the not the dark we fear,
Not the whisper in our ear,

Not the hate in our heart,
Not the pain of being apart,

The fire that burns,
Not the mind that learns,

The loss of what we've gained,
The emotions that we've named,

We are our experiences,
We are our pain,
We are our joy,
We are our hate,
We are our love,
We are our kindness,

We are what we do, what we say.

We are who we are,
And that should be enough.

Colour in the Wood

In what do colours reside?
The plume of wild catastrophe,

What do we request of daisies?
It flowers, it blooms,

In what do colours reside?
Representing nothing, but its former glory,

It was precious for far too long,
So now it resides,
As a shadow of its former self,

In the thicket it hides,
The flower in which colour resides,

The Grinning Crow

It grinned at me,
The crow,
It smiled callously,
Knowingly,
For what secret I hold,
Are not secrets to him,

He knows and he smiles,
As I blush and I scowl,
The crow,
That crow,
He knows,
And may not tell,

He may not tell,
But he surely could,
Though they are not his to tell,
I wish I could tell him,
But he knows,

He grinned at me,
For he knew,
For I knew,
The secrets I hold,
Are the secrets he told,

Choice

It matters not what I see, or hear, or taste, or touch,

My senses do what they are meant to do,

They speak to me,

That thing is beautiful,
This thing is poisonous,

And then I have a choice,

Do I shut my eyes or lay them on the beautiful?
Do I pour out the poison or do I drink?

Pain, Gain, Sweat Stain

Vile, and frigid the crime,

Bitter, an anti-quitter,

A toxin of Society,

She stones her nose,

And where it goes,

Pain of all kinds, are sure to follow,

I watch,

I fantasise,

But never comes the day,

When I get to say,

"SHUT THE FUCK UP!"

The Void

I was there and it was not a pleasant stay,

With the pain jolting me, I am transported,

My creativity confined to a filing cabinet,

And when I open it a shock to my jaw, like a punch,

Again, a punch,

Again,

Again,

I shall find my muse before I sleep,

"You shall not keep me from that which is mine.",

Demon pain,

My state of Becoming locked away,

In a filing cabinet.

Winter's Gone

It is and it isn't,
Conceivably so,
This world that spins,
Above and below,

In treating my mind to a meal of words,
To devour,
Such sour,
Devotee blurbs,

It is and it isn't,
Decidedly so,
A winter takes summer,
Into an inspired icy glow,

So,
When the wind blows East,
And the Sun buried deep,
The moon rises up,
Putting the day to sleep.

For Not a Better Word

Could and Should are one in the same,

If one has the money, if one has the means,

I have neither, but new found holes in my concrete jeans,

If only I could bathe,

Perhaps I would not feel my situation so grave,

I am left to my own devices in this state,

My feast is the yeast built up on your discarded plate.

Clothes

I do not know my size,
For it had never fit me, to fit in them,

Baggy has never suited me,
But I have yet to give it up,

Baggy means "Lazy" in some languages,
In others it means "Worldly"
Though the fabric must be thin.

I do not buy for the brand,
Or,
For what it will do to my figure,

I might stare begrudgingly into a mirror some days,
Disappointment communicated through my furrowed brow,

Most days though,
My skirt does fit,
My shirt is slimming,
My jacket is fly,
And I feel damn good.

To you I am?

To be alone with you
if only for a moment
a crime a tears, beyond,
no where to go because the destination
If here in your whole, in your heart, I am here
And yet, so far apart, I am not,

I am not your destination and it seems so far
No matter how close our evening star.
I can't help but think that I am in the way,
Of the true star you seek,

I'm in the way, but not?

Who am I any longer to you if not the goal?

I am no longer the goal,
For I have been reached,
Now I am on the shelf,
A trophy of a time out of reach,
Here,
I am a goal no longer,

And you no longer seek me,
For I am here.

I Saw That Day

I saw her,
I knew him,
I'd seen them,

Her beautiful red skin,
His towering horns,
Their impatient tail,

See, it did not matter,
Not, "What".
But, "Who".

Not the flesh,
The grace,
Not the blush,
The face,

There to purchase,
From a sinister place,
There to play,
And I was in the way.

Shared Memories

I don't know how they are read,
These words from my head,

I write them on the page,
For those of any age,

To comprehend their meaning instead,

I don't know how they are read,
These words of mine,

Are they fast?
Are they slow?
Are they mid range prose?

For after they are written,
They are no longer just mine,

They are a lover,
A good day,
A bad day,
And a kind friend,

I don't know how these words are read,
Because they are not mine.

No Shoes

I've got a pair of shoes,
a pair of pants,
a pair of underwear,
But I do not like them,

I belong to the wild,
And the wild doesn't wear shoes,

I should be naked,
Laying in a grassy meadow somewhere,
Not wearing shoes,

I should be running along the beach,
The wind in my hair,
Not wearing shoes,

Society says I should wear clothes,
I should really be naked,
Not wearing shoes,

I should be in a garden of flowers,
Blooming above the buds,
And not wearing shoes,

I have a pair of shoes,

A pair of pants,
A pair of underwear,
A t shirt,
A jacket,
And sometimes a hat,

But really I should be naked.

Wolves

The wolves are coming and they will have my hands,
Digits, divided, and devoured,

The wolves are coming and they shall have my eyes,
And they shall see truths beyond the veil,

The wolves are coming and they shall have my teeth,
And they shall tell grand stories when they speak,

The wolves are coming and they will have my ears,
And they will take words with understanding,

They wolves are coming and they will have my feet,
And they will feel the cold between my toes,

The wolves are coming,
And I am what sustains their journey

Power

There are days when you are a Princess,
A Prince of many,
There are days when you are a Queen,
Or a King of old,
There are days when you wear a crown,

Then there are days where the crown wears you.

My Art

I am different,
Unrefined and restrained,
Held back by my fear of failure,

But I shall fall and fail if I pretend be someone
I am not,
I must set myself free,
Release, release,

Fall on purpose,
Grow and climb from the bottom where I was before,

So now who am I?
What am I?

My art,
What makes it?

How does it stand apart?

I am myself, restrained,
So I must be freed,
Only then will my art be me.

My Journey

It's a vessel,
A tireless contraption,
Telling me to press on,

And I shall listen,
What choice do I have?
We must move together,
To forward OUR goals,

It is as you say a meat puppet,
Stumbling through a disenchanted forest,
Of concrete grass and steel beam trees,

Yes, it is a vessel,
But it is mine and mine alone,
And I shall do with it what I wish,

If that means in the end,
my strings are cut and I am missing toes,
Then so be it,

For I puppeteered with passion,
Enjoying every moment.

It's All Gone

Pardon Me,
For I appear to have lost my mind,

My Patience,
My Kindness
My Joy,

Pardon my thoughtlessness,
But I can't find my brain,

My Ideas,
My Structure,
My Process,

Pardon my Forgetfulness,
It seems I have misplaced my marbles,

My Creativity,
My Projects,
My Muse,

It will be back,
But until then,

I beg your pardon,

I have apparently forgotten myself.

Ever Faster

It's faster, faster,
It goes everywhere faster,
Until it's. Just. Gone.

You and me

It's hard to breathe without me,
Without you it is hard to see,

The stars are bright,
And you are my light,

In my world of you.

Choices

The lesser of two evils,
The largest of two weevils,

Lose or win,
Sink or swim,
When difficulty comes crawling.

In regards to Woe

Don't blame the snake,
Don't blame the man,

Blame those who get away with anything they can,

Who try to distract from the hate and the pain by simply saying "In God's Name".

I must interrupt your regularly scheduled poetry to try something a little new. I gathered a collection of poetry from my friends and family who wished to participate. So without further ado, please enjoy the following poetry from my lovely friends and family.

Some may have asked to remain anonymous so I have signed those poems as O.W.S.(One Who Shares)

Ferryman

Here i am
Floating on the water again,
The air is silent and still
The fog hangs heavy and the night envelopes all
The endlessness, i hear her call
Again, I set sail to reach nothingness
She calls like siren
Dragging me back to the boat
She bids me
Ferry my soul

Ferryman, Ferryman

The void beckons

Slipping slipping
No longer watching each step
Not a fall
Not a surrender
Walking, walking into the end
The mind had no thought
The eyes are blinded to all
And alone and unguided
The gate is closer
Running as if escaping
But running straight to a cage
Unravelling,
Unravelling
No chance to turn around

Dead garden

In the garden i wanted to grow
I planted the seed,
But what do I sow?
Just shrivelled up failures of what might have bee
There dead dried flowers
Never given a chance,
I choked their roots and they twisted up together
Gave them none of my water
For it served someone better
Because my garden isn't grand or beautiful or full
I know how to tend it but this is the key
I won't tend to my garden if it's for me

Me, Me.

I tell stories
I weave them together
With threads of my own
The people i meet
The places i've seen
For every heart holds one
Mundane or exciting
Every life, is a story worth writing

Tales of love, or heartbreak
Trepidation and pain
Ballands of creation, and not one is the same
A saga of triumph, laden with hardship and aches
A song full of rejoicing and the courage it takes

The ones i lost
The ones i hold
The ones best forgotten
Tales yet to unfold
I braid together this tapestry of me

And everything i have heard and seen
I gather my courage and return to the dream
To live without fear and love without question
This story is mine, and it's brilliant you see
Because its built from the parts
That make me, me

To the newly discovered x-ray
lights from behind the far side of
a black hole 800 million light
years away proving the theory
that immense concentrations of
matter can bend the fabric of
spacetime

And all at once, a light behind was seen.
As if you sat atop the world
alone. But being, not yet lonesome

Afterward

This Afterward was just as difficult to write as the introduction. I had so many thoughts and depending on the point of life I was in, it was clear I was simply using the end of this book as a much needed therapist.

In the end there is only really one thing left to say and that is "Thank you". Thank you to those who supported me, thank you to those who added their own poetry to the mix and thank you to everyone who bought and loved a copy of this pocket book of poetry.